Dear Jennifer,

Best Wishes to you as you begin the most rewarding and sometimes frustrating journey in your life! :)

Love,
Marilyn, Kim
& Ida

for mothers everywhere,

in loving appreciation

and much admiration

Especially for Mothers

HELEN STEINER RICE

A DayMaker Greeting Book

*O*f all the books ever written no one knows how many have been dedicated to mothers. But everyone knows why. ✍ She's a best friend, physician, strong support, and advocate. She's the cozy comforter and the bowl of chicken soup, but also her children's mirror and conscience. The little voice inside that still proffers good advice no matter how old or wise her children think they've become. She's the first on her knees in the morning and, throughout the day, brings the needs of her children before her heavenly Father. ✍ *Especially for Mothers* is a special collection of poetry by Helen Steiner Rice and is dedicated to mothers everywhere. From a woman cradling her first child or grandchild, and the mother standing her ground against a strong-willed toddler or teenager, to teary-eyed and unabashedly proud women at crowning moments in their children's lives, these words of love and inspiration are for you. ✍ The poems of Helen Steiner Rice have been cherished by millions for over five decades. While the peace, joy, and love of the Christian life, the splendor of nature, and God's comfort in times of sorrow are the themes of her verses, Rice seems to have saved her deepest emotions for poems about mothers.

A Mother's Love

Mother

You're the answer to

and the symbol of what is marriage

and what is love!

In all this world, through all of time,

There could not be another

Who could fulfill God's purpose

As completely as a mother!

WHAT IS A MOTHER?

It takes a mother's love
    to make a house a home,
A place to be remembered,
    no matter where we roam.
It takes a mother's patience
    to bring a child up right,
And her courage and her cheerfulness
    to make a dark day bright.
It takes a mother's thoughtfulness
    to mend the heart's deep "hurts,"
And her skill and her endurance
    to mend little socks and shirts.
It takes a mother's kindness
    to forgive us when we err,
To sympathize in trouble
    and bow her head in prayer.
It takes a mother's wisdom
    to recognize our needs
And to give us reassurance
    by her loving words and deeds.

MOTHER IS A WORD CALLED LOVE

Mother is a word called love
And all the world is mindful of
The love that's given and shown to others
Is different from the love of mothers.
For mothers play the leading roles
In giving birth to little souls,
For though small souls are heaven-sent
And we realize they're only lent,
It takes a mother's loving hands
And her gentle heart that understands
To mold and shape this little life
And shelter it through storm and strife.
So mothers are a special race
God sent to earth to take His place,
And mother is a lovely name
That even saints are proud to claim.

PEACE BEGINS IN THE HOME AND THE HEART

Peace is not something you fight for
With bombs and missiles that kill,
Nor can it be won in a "battle of words"
Man fashions by scheming and skill...
For men who are greedy and warlike,
Whose avarice for power cannot cease,
Can never contribute in helping
To bring this world nearer to peace...
For in seeking peace for all people
There is only one place to begin
And that is in each home and heart—
For the fortress of peace is within!

MOTHERHOOD

The dearest gifts that heaven holds,
The very finest, too,
Were made into one pattern
That was perfect, sweet and true;
The angels smiled, well pleased, and said:
"Compared to all the others,
This pattern is so wonderful
Let's use it just for mothers!"
And through the years, a mother
Has been all that's sweet and good
For there's a bit of God and love,
In all true motherhood.

NEVER BORROW SORROW

Deal only with the present,
Never step into tomorrow,
For God asks us just to trust Him
And to never borrow sorrow—
For the future is not ours to know
And it may never be,
So let us live and give our best
And give it lavishly—
For to meet tomorrow's troubles
Before they are even ours
Is to anticipate the Saviour
And to doubt His all-wise powers—
So let us be content to solve
Our problems one by one,
Asking nothing of tomorrow
Except Thy will be done.

TWO PALESTINIAN SEAS
One is a sparking sapphire jewel,
Its waters are clean and clear and cool,
Along its shores the children play
And travelers seek it on their way,
And nature gives so lavishly
Her choicest gems to the Galilee...
But on to the south the Jordan flows
Into a sea where nothing grows,
No splash of fish, no singing bird,
No children's laughter is ever heard,
The air hangs heavy all around
And nature shuns this barren ground...
Both seas receive the Jordan's flow,
The water is just the same, we know,
But one of the seas, like liquid sun,
Can warm the hearts of everyone,
While farther south another sea
Is dead and dark and miserly—
It takes each drop the Jordan brings
And to each drop it fiercely clings...
It hoards and holds the Jordan's waves
Until like shackled, captured slaves
The fresh, clear Jordan turns to salt
And dies within the Dead Sea's vault...

But the Jordan flows on rapturously
As it enters and leaves the Galilee,
For every drop that the Jordan gives
Becomes a laughing wave that lives—
For the Galilee gives back each drop,
Its waters flow and never stop,
And in this laughing, living sea
That takes and gives so generously
We find the way to Life and Living
Is not in Keeping, but in Giving!

Yes, there are Two Palestinian Seas
And mankind is fashioned after these!

MY LOVE FOR YOU
There are things we cannot measure,
Like the depths of waves and sea
And the heights of stars in heaven
And the joy you bring to me...
Like eternity's long endlessness
And the sunset's golden hue,
There is no way to measure
The love I have for you.

FOR MOTHER
ON MOTHER'S DAY
No other love
Than mother love
Could do the things
Required of
The one to whom
God gives the keeping
Of His wee lambs,
Awake or sleeping.

A
Mother's faith

No Hands Are Empty

What can I do? I've so little to give,

How can I show someone else how to live

When I hardly know how to manage my day?

But I plead with my heart,

Teach me to pray!

MY DAILY PRAYER

God, be my resting place and my protection
In hours of trouble, defeat, and dejection...
May I never give way to self-pity and sorrow,
May I always be sure of a better tomorrow,
May I stand undaunted come what may
Secure in my knowledge I have only to pray
And ask my Creator and Father above
To keep me serene in His grace and His love!

A Mother's Faith

It is a mother's faith
In our Father above
That fills the home with happiness
And the heart with truth and love!

A Sure Way to a Happy Day

Happiness is something
    we create in our mind,
It's not something you search for
    and so seldom find—
It's just waking up
    and beginning the day
By counting our blessings
    and kneeling to pray—
It's giving up thoughts
    that breed discontent
And accepting what comes
    as a "gift heaven-sent"—
It's giving up wishing
    for things we have not
And making the best of
    whatever we've got—
It's knowing that life
    is determined for us,
And pursuing our tasks
—without fret, fume or fuss—
For it's by completing
    what God gives us to do
That we find real contentment
    and happiness, too.

A Mother's Love Is a Haven in the Storm of Life

A mother's love is like an island
In life's ocean vast and wide,
A peaceful, quiet shelter
From the restless, rising tide.

A mother's love is like a fortress
And we seek protection there
When the waves of tribulation
Seem to drown us in despair.

A mother's love is a sanctuary
Where our souls can find sweet rest
From the struggle and the tension
Of life's fast and futile quest.

A mother's love is like a tower
Rising far above the crowd,
And her smile is like the sunshine
Breaking through a threatening cloud.

A mother's love is like a beacon
Burning bright with faith and prayer.
And through the changing scenes of life
We can find a haven there.

For a mother's love is fashioned
After God's enduring love,
It is endless and unfailing
Like the love of Him above.

For God knew in His great wisdom
That He couldn't be everywhere,
So He put His little children
In a loving mother's care.

A Mother's Day Prayer

Our Father in heaven
   whose love is divine,
Thanks for the love
   of a mother like mine—
And in Thy great mercy
   look down from above
And grant this dear mother
   the gift of Your love—
And all through the year,
   whatever betide her,
Assure her each day
   that You are beside her—
And, Father in heaven,
   show me the way
To lighten her tasks
   and brighten her day,
And bless her dear heart
   with the insight to see
That her love means more
   than the world to me.

A Child's Faith

"Jesus loves me, this I know,
For the Bible tells me so"
Little children ask no more,
For love is all they're looking for,
And in a small child's shining eyes
The Faith of all the ages lies
And tiny hands and tousled heads
That kneel in prayer by little beds
Are closer to the dear Lord's heart
And of His Kingdom more a part
Than we who search, and never find,
The answers to our questioning mind.
For Faith in things we cannot see
Requires a child's simplicity.

A Prayer for Those We Love

"Our Father who art in heaven,"
Hear this little prayer
And reach across the miles today
That stretch from here to there,
So I may feel much closer
To those I'm fondest of
And they may know I think of them
With thankfulness and love,
And help all people everywhere
Who must often dwell apart
To know that they're together
In the haven of the heart!

The Joy of Unselfish Giving

Time is not measured
    by the years that you live
But by the deeds that you do
    and the joy that you give—
And each day as it comes
    brings a chance to each one
To love to the fullest,
    leaving nothing undone
That would brighten the life
    or lighten the load
Of some weary traveler
    lost on life's road—
So what does it matter
    how long we may live
If as long as we live
    we unselfishly give.

Her Fragrance

"flowers leave their fragrance on the hand that bestows them"

There's an old Chinese proverb
  that, if practiced each day,
Would change the whole world
  in a wonderful way—
Its truth is so simple,
  it's so easy to do,
And it works every time
  and successfully, too—
For you can't do a kindness
  without a reward,
Not in silver nor gold
  but in joy from the Lord—
You can't light a candle
  to show others the way

Without feeling the warmth
    of that bright little ray—
And you can't pluck a rose,
    all fragrant with dew,
Without part of its fragrance
    remaining with you...
And whose hands bestow
    more fragrant bouquets
Than Mother who daily
    speaks kind words of praise?
A Mother whose courage
    and comfort and cheer
Lights bright little candles
    in hearts through the year—
No wonder the hands
    of an unselfish mother
Are symbols of sweetness
    unlike any other.

Walking with God

WHO CULTIVATES A GARDEN

AND GROWS FLOWERS FROM THE SOD,

WALKS HAND IN HAND WITH NATURE

AND VERY CLOSE TO GOD.

LIFE'S FAIREST FLOWER

I have a garden within my soul
Of wondrous beauty rare,
Wherein the blossoms of my life
Bloom ever in splendor fair.

The fragrance and charm of that garden,
Where all of life's flowers bloom,
Fills my aching heart with sweet content
And banishes failure's gloom.

Each flower a message is bringing,
A memory of someone dear,
A picture of deepest devotion,
Dispelling all doubt and fear.

Amid all this beauty and splendor,
One flower stands forth as queen,
Alone in her dazzling beauty,
Alone but ever supreme.

This flower of love and devotion
Has guided me all through life,
Softening my grief and my sorrow,
Sharing my toil and my strife.

This flower has helped me to conquer
Temptation so black and grim
And led me to victory and honor
Over my enemy, sin.

I have vainly sought in my garden,
Through blossoms of love and light,
For a flower of equal wonder
To compare with this one so bright.

But ever I've met with failure,
My search has been in vain,
For never a flower existed,
Like the blossom I can claim.

For after years I now can see,
Amid life's roses and rue,
God's greatest gift to a little child,
My darling mother, was you.

MOTHER'S DAY

Mother's Day is remembrance day
And we pause on the path of the year
To pay honor and worshipful tribute
To the mother our heart holds dear...
For, whether here or in heaven,
Her love is our haven and guide,
For always the memory of mother
Is a beacon light shining inside...
Time cannot destroy her memory
And years can never erase
The tenderness and the beauty
Of the love in a mother's face...
And, when we think of our mother,
We draw nearer to God above,
For only God in His greatness
Could fashion a mother's love.

Always There

"The House of Prayer"

"THE HOUSE OF PRAYER" IS NO FARTHER AWAY

THAN THE QUIET SPOT WHERE YOU KNEEL AND PRAY,

FOR THE HEART IS A TEMPLE WHEN GOD IS THERE

AS YOU PLACE YOURSELF IN HIS LOVING CARE.

WITH GOD ALL
THINGS ARE POSSIBLE!
Nothing is ever too hard to do
If your faith is strong
and your purpose it true...
So never give up and never stop
Just journey on to the mountaintop!

At My Mother's Knee

I have worshiped in churches and chapels
I have prayed in the busy street.
I have sought my God and have found Him
Where the waves of the ocean beat.
I have knelt in a silent forest
In the shade of an ancient tree.
But the dearest of all my altars
Was raised at my mother's knee.
God make me the woman of her vision
And purge me of all selfishness
And keep me true to her standards
And help me to live to bless
And then keep me a pilgrim forever
At the shrine of my mother's knee.

There Is a Reason for Everything

Our Father knows what's best for us,
    so why should we complain?
We always want the sunshine,
    but He knows there must be rain.
We love the sound of laughter
    and the merriment of cheer,
But our hearts would lose their tenderness
    if we never shed a tear.
Our Father tests us often
    with suffering and with sorrow.
He tests us not to punish us
    but to help us with tomorrow.
For growing trees are strengthened
    when they withstand the storm,
And the sharp cut of a chisel
    gives the marble grace and form.
God never hurts us needlessly,
    and He never wastes our pain,
For every loss He sends to us
    is followed by rich gain.
And when we count the blessings
    that God has so freely sent,
We will find no cause for murmuring
    and no time to lament,
For our Father loves His children,
    and to Him all things are plain,
So He never sends us pleasure
    when the soul's deep need is pain.
So whenever we are troubled
    and when everything goes wrong,
It is just God working in us
    to make our spirits strong.

The Faith to Believe

What must I do
    to insure peace of mind?
Is the answer I'm seeking
    too hard to find?
How can I know
    what God wants me to be?
How can I tell
    what's expected of me?
Where can I go
    for guidance and aid
To help me correct
    the errors I've made
The answer is found
    in doing three things,
And great is the gladness
    that doing them brings...
Do justice, love kindness,
    walk humbly with God.
For with these three things
    as your rule and your rod,
All things worth having
    are yours to achieve
If you follow God's words
    and have faith to believe.

THIS, TOO, WILL PASS AWAY

If I can endure for this minute
Whatever is happening to me,
No matter how heavy my heart is
Or how dark the moment may be—
If I can remain calm and quiet
With all my world crashing about me,
Secure in the knowledge God loves me
When everyone else seems to doubt me—
If I can but keep on believing
What I know in my heart to be true,
That darkness will fade with the morning
And that this will pass away, too—
Then nothing in life can defeat me
For as long as this knowledge remains
I can suffer whatever is happening
For I know God will break all the chains
That are binding me tight in the darkness
And trying to fill me with fear—
For there is no night without dawning
And I know that my morning is near.

She Gives So Much

WHERE THERE IS LOVE

Where there is love the heart it light,
Where there is love the day is bright,
Where there is love there is a song
To help when things are going wrong...
Where there is love there is a smile
To make all things seem more worthwhile.
Where there is love there's quiet peace,
A tranquil place where turmoils cease...
Love changes darkness into light
And makes the heart take "wingless flight"...
And Mothers have a special way
Of filling homes with love each day,
And when the home is filled with love
You'll always find God spoken of,
And when a family "prays together"
That family also "stays together"...
And once again a Mother's touch
Can mold and shape and do so much
To make this world a better place
For every color, creed and race—
For when man walks with God again,
There shall be Peace on Earth for Men.

*God,
Grant Me...*

COURAGE AND HOPE FOR EVERY DAY,

FAITH TO GUIDE ME ALONG MY WAY,

UNDERSTANDING AND WISDOM, TOO,

AND GRACE TO ACCEPT

WHAT LIFE GIVES ME TO DO.

Why Am I Complaining?

My cross is not too heavy,
My road is not too rough
Because God walks beside me
And to know this is enough...
And though I get so lonely
I know I'm not alone
For the Lord God is my Father
And He loves me as His own...
So let me stop complaining
About my "load of care"
For God will always lighten it
When it gets too much to bear...
And if He does not ease my load
He will give me strength to bear it
For God in love and mercy
Is always near to share it.

The Reflections of God

The silent stars in timeless skies,
The wonderment in children's eyes,
The gossamer wings of a hummingbird,
The joy that comes from a kindly word.
The autumn haze, the breath of spring,
The chirping song the crickets sing,
A rosebud in a slender vase
Are all reflections of God's face.

No Favor Do I Seek Today

I come not to ask,
    to please or implore You,
I just come to tell You
    how much I adore You,
For to kneel in Your Presence
    makes me feel blest
For I know that You
    know all my needs best...
And it fills me with joy
    just to linger with You
For prayer is much more
    than just asking for things—
It's the peace and contentment
    that quietness brings...
So thank You again
    for Your mercy and love
And for making me heir
    to Your kingdom above!

Darling Mother

Life's Richest Treasure

LIFE'S RICHEST TREASURE

THAT MONEY CANNOT MEASURE

IS A MOTHER'S LOVE,

A HEART GIFT FROM GOD ABOVE.

IDEALS ARE LIKE STARS

In this world of casual carelessness
  it's discouraging to try
To keep our morals and standards
  and our ideals high...
We are ridiculed and laughed at
  by the smart sophisticate
Who proclaims in brittle banter
  that such things are out of date...
But no life is worth the living
  unless it's built on truth,
And we lay our life's foundation
  in the golden years of youth...
So allow no one to stop you
  or hinder you from laying
A firm and strong foundation
  made of Faith and Love and Praying. . .
For High Ideals are like the Stars
  that light the sky above...
You cannot ever reach them,
  but lift your heart up high
And your life will be as shining
  as the stars up in the sky.

A MOTHER'S LOVE

A mother's love is something
   that no one can explain,
It is made of deep devotion
   and of sacrifice and pain,
It is endless and unselfish
   and enduring come what may
For nothing can destroy it
   or take that love away...
It is patient and forgiving
   when all others are forsaking,
And it never fails or falters
   even though the heart is breaking...
It believes beyond believing
   when the world around condemns,
And it glows with all the beauty
   of the rarest, brightest gems...
It is far beyond defining,
   it defies all explanation,
And it still remains a secret
   like the mysteries of creation...
A many splendored miracle
   man cannot understand
And another wondrous evidence
   of God's tender guiding hand.

MOTHER'S ADVICE

Sometimes when a light
goes out of our life
and we are left in darkness
and do not know which way to go.
we must put our hand
into the hand of God
and ask Him to lead us...
and if we let our life
become a prayer
until we are strong enough
to stand under the weight
of our own thoughts again,
somehow even the most difficult
hours are bearable.

WONDROUS EVIDENCE

Who can see
the dawn break through
without a glimpse
of Heaven and You...
For who but God
could make the day
and gently put
the night away.

A
Mother's Prayer

Now I Lay Me Down to Sleep

I remember so well this prayer I said
Each night as my mother tucked me in bed.
And today this same prayer is still the best way
To "sign off with God" at the end of the day.
Ask Him your soul to safely keep
As you wearily close your tired eyes in sleep
Feeling content that the Father above
Will hold you secure in His strong arms of love.
Having His promise that if ere you wake,
His angels will reach down, your sweet soul to take,
Is perfect assurance that awake or asleep,
God is always right there to tenderly keep
All of His children ever safe in His care.
So into His hands each night as I sleep,
I commend my soul for the dear Lord to keep.
Knowing that if my soul should take flight,
It will soar to the land where there is no night.

For after years I now can see,

Amid life's roses and rue,

God's greatest gift to a little child,

My darling mother, was you.

DayMaker
GREETING BOOKS

© 2003 by Barbour Publishing, Inc.

All poems © The Helen Steiner Rice Foundation
All rights reserved.

ISBN 1-58660-703-0

Cover images: ©Steven Puetzer Photonica
Book design by Kevin Keller/ designconcepts

Published by Barbour Books, an imprint of Barbour Publishing, Inc.,
P.O. Box 719, Uhrichsville, Ohio 44683, www.barbourbooks.com

Member of the
Evangelical Christian
Publishers Association

Printed in China.

5 4 3 2 1